Korean Men and Love

A Western Woman's Guide to Dating and Relationships

Introduction to Korean Men

Welcome to our book about dating and building relationships with Korean men! We are a happy couple, with him being a Korean man and her being a western woman. Throughout our relationship, we have faced and overcome many challenges related to our cultural differences, and we wanted to share our insights and experiences with others who may be navigating similar situations.

As our world becomes increasingly globalized, more and more people are finding love across cultural boundaries. While this can be an exciting and enriching experience, it can also present unique challenges related to communication, expectations, and values. We have written this book to provide guidance, support, and advice for anyone who is interested in building a successful relationship with a Korean man.

In this book, we will explore traditional and modern dating customs in Korea, as well as expectations and norms for initiating and pursuing relationships. We will discuss differences in communication styles, personality traits, and attitudes towards intimacy and commitment. We will also provide practical tips for navigating cultural differences, building trust and understanding, and sustaining passion and fulfillment in your relationship.

Whether you are currently in a relationship with a Korean man or simply interested in learning more about Korean culture and dating customs, this book is for you. We hope that our insights and experiences will help you navigate the complexities of cross-cultural relationships and build a happy and fulfilling life with your partner.

Dating Culture in Korea

Overview of Traditional Dating Customs in Korea

Korean dating culture has a rich history and unique traditions that have been shaped by the country's cultural and social norms. From traditional matchmaking to modern dating apps, Korean dating customs have evolved over time, but they still retain many of their traditional elements. In this chapter, we will provide an overview of traditional dating customs in Korea, to help readers understand and appreciate this unique aspect of Korean culture.

Arranged Marriage

Historically, arranged marriages were common in Korea, particularly among the upper classes. Matchmakers would often play a key role in bringing together eligible candidates, taking into account factors such as family background, social status, and compatibility. While arranged marriages are less common today, many Korean families still place a strong emphasis on finding a suitable partner for their children.

Meeting and Dating

In traditional Korean dating culture, couples would often meet through mutual acquaintances or introductions. Once a couple began dating, they would typically go on chaperoned dates, accompanied by friends or family members. Physical contact was often limited, and couples would take things slow to build trust and respect.

Confession and Acceptance

In traditional Korean dating culture, a confession of love was an important step in a relationship. A man would typically confess his feelings to a woman through a written letter, which would be delivered by a friend or family member. If the woman accepted the confession, they would become a couple.

Dinner and Gift Giving

In traditional Korean dating culture, dinner dates were often an important part of a relationship. Couples would typically go out to eat at a nice restaurant, with the man paying for the meal. Gift giving was also an important part of dating culture, with couples exchanging small tokens of affection, such as flowers or chocolates.

Family Approval

In traditional Korean dating culture, family approval was often a key factor in a relationship. Couples would seek the approval of each other's families before becoming serious, and the families would often play an important role in the relationship, offering advice and support.

Traditional Korean dating customs are a reflection of the country's unique cultural and social norms. From arranged marriages to chaperoned dates, these customs have evolved over time, but they still retain many of their traditional elements. By understanding and appreciating these customs, readers can gain a deeper appreciation for Korean culture and better connect with the Korean men they meet.

Comparison of Modern Dating Practices in Korea and the West

Modern dating practices in Korea and the West have evolved in different ways, influenced by cultural, social, and technological factors. While both cultures share some similarities, such as the use of dating apps, there are also significant differences in the way dating is approached and practiced. In this chapter, we will compare modern dating practices in Korea and the West, to help readers better understand and appreciate the similarities and differences.

Dating Apps

Dating apps have become increasingly popular in both Korea and the West, providing a convenient way for people to meet potential partners. In Korea, the most popular dating app is Tinder, while in the West, apps such as Bumble and Hinge are also popular. However, there are some differences in the way dating apps are used in each culture. In Korea, it is common for users to include their blood type in their dating profiles, as this is believed to reveal personality traits. In the West, users may be more focused on including photos and information about their interests and hobbies.

Casual Dating

Casual dating is more common in the West than in Korea, where relationships tend to be more serious and long-term. In the West, it is not uncommon for people to date multiple partners at the same time, or to engage in casual hookups. In Korea, however, dating is often seen as a precursor to marriage, and couples are expected to be exclusive and committed to each other.

Public Displays of Affection

Public displays of affection are more accepted and common in the West than in Korea, where it is considered more appropriate to keep physical affection private. Holding hands and kissing in public are not as common in Korea, and couples are more likely to show affection through small gestures, such as holding hands under the table.

Meeting the Family

In both Korea and the West, meeting the family is an important step in a relationship. However, the timing and significance of this step may differ. In Korea, meeting the family is often seen as a serious commitment, and is reserved for more serious relationships. In the West, meeting the family may happen earlier in the relationship and may not carry the same weight of commitment.

Expectations and Norms for Initiating and Pursuing Relationships in Korea

Korean dating culture has its own unique set of expectations and norms when it comes to initiating and pursuing relationships. While there are no hard and fast rules, there are certain cultural and social norms that are important to understand when dating Korean men. In this chapter, we will explore the expectations and norms for initiating and pursuing relationships in Korea, to help readers navigate the dating scene with confidence and cultural sensitivity.

Initiating Relationships

In Korean dating culture, it is generally expected that the man will take the lead in initiating a relationship. This means that men are expected to ask women out on dates, make the first move in physical contact, and generally take the lead in pursuing the relationship. However, this does not mean that women are passive or uninvolved in the relationship. Women are often expected to reciprocate the man's interest and communicate their feelings through nonverbal cues.

Courtship

In Korean dating culture, courtship is a key part of initiating and pursuing a relationship. Courtship involves getting to know each other on a deeper level and building trust and respect. This may involve going on chaperoned dates, spending time with each other's families, and engaging in meaningful conversations about shared interests and values.

Communication

Effective communication is important in any relationship, and this is especially true in Korean dating culture. Korean men place a strong emphasis on communication and expect their partners to be open and honest with them. This means being direct and clear in expressing one's feelings and expectations, as well as listening actively and empathetically to the other person.

Cultural Norms

Korean dating culture is heavily influenced by cultural and social norms, and it is important to be aware of these norms when dating Korean men. For example, public displays of affection are generally less common and less accepted in Korea than in the West. It is also important to be aware of traditional gender roles and expectations, such as men being expected to provide for their families and women being expected to take care of the home.

Initiating and pursuing relationships in Korea is influenced by a variety of cultural, social, and historical factors. Understanding the expectations and norms for dating in Korea is essential for building strong and successful relationships with Korean men. By being aware of these expectations and norms, readers can navigate the dating scene with cultural sensitivity and build strong and meaningful connections with the Korean men they meet.

Dating Etiquette with Korean Men

How to Approach and Express Interest in a Korean Man

Approaching and expressing interest in a Korean man can be intimidating, especially if you are unfamiliar with Korean dating culture. However, with the right approach and understanding of cultural norms, it is possible to connect with Korean men and build strong and meaningful relationships. In this chapter, we will provide tips on how to approach and express interest in a Korean man, to help readers navigate the dating scene with confidence and cultural sensitivity.

1. Be Confident

Confidence is key when approaching and expressing interest in a Korean man. Korean men tend to value confidence and assertiveness in their partners, so it is important to approach them with a positive and confident attitude. This can involve initiating conversations, asking questions, and expressing interest in their hobbies and interests.

2. Show Interest in Korean Culture

Showing an interest in Korean culture can be a great way to connect with Korean men and demonstrate your cultural sensitivity. This can involve learning about Korean cuisine, music, or history, and sharing your own experiences and interests as well. This can help to create a shared sense of cultural understanding and appreciation, which is an important foundation for any relationship.

3. Be Respectful

Respect is a key value in Korean culture, and it is important to show respect when approaching and expressing interest in a Korean man. This can involve being polite, using formal language when appropriate, and being mindful of cultural norms and expectations. It is also important to be respectful of their personal space and boundaries, and to avoid making assumptions or stereotypes about Korean men.

4. Be Honest and Direct

Korean men value honesty and directness in their partners, so it is important to be clear and upfront about your intentions and feelings. This can involve expressing your interest in the person, as well as communicating your expectations and boundaries. It is important to be respectful and considerate in your communication, but also to be honest and direct about your feelings and desires.

5. Use Nonverbal Cues

Nonverbal communication is an important part of Korean dating culture, and using nonverbal cues can be a great way to express interest in a Korean man. This can involve making eye contact, smiling, and using appropriate body language. It is also important to be mindful of cultural norms around physical touch and public displays of affection, and to be respectful of the other person's personal boundaries.

Approaching and expressing interest in a Korean man can be challenging, but with the right approach and understanding of cultural norms, it is possible to build strong and meaningful relationships. By being confident, respectful, honest, and direct, and by using appropriate nonverbal cues, readers can navigate the dating scene with cultural sensitivity and build meaningful connections with the Korean men they meet.

Appropriate Ways to Show Affection in Public in Korea

Public displays of affection are less common and less accepted in Korean dating culture than in the West. Korean society places a strong emphasis on respect, modesty, and maintaining personal boundaries, and public displays of affection may be seen as inappropriate or disrespectful. However, there are still ways to show affection in public that are appropriate and acceptable in Korean dating culture. In this chapter, we will explore appropriate ways to show affection in public in Korea, to help readers navigate the dating scene with cultural sensitivity and respect.

1. Holding Hands

Holding hands is a common and acceptable way to show affection in public in Korea. This can involve walking hand in hand, or sitting close together with your hands touching. Holding hands is seen as a sign of commitment and affection, and is generally considered acceptable in most public settings.

2. Arm in Arm

Walking arm in arm is another way to show affection in public in Korea. This involves linking arms with your partner and walking together. This is a common way for couples to show their commitment and affection for each other, without being overly physical or intimate.

3. Hugs

Hugs are generally considered acceptable in Korean dating culture, as long as they are not overly long or intimate. Quick hugs or side hugs are generally more acceptable than full frontal hugs, which may be seen as too intimate in public.

4. Small Gestures

Small gestures, such as touching your partner's arm or shoulder, can also be a way to show affection in public in Korea. These gestures are generally seen as non-threatening and non-sexual, and can be a way to show your partner that you care without being overly physical.

5. Respect Cultural Norms

It is important to respect cultural norms and expectations when showing affection in public in Korea. Public displays of affection, such as kissing or hugging, may be seen as inappropriate or disrespectful in certain contexts, such as in front of elders or in religious settings. It is important to be aware of these cultural norms and to be respectful of others when showing affection in public.

Taboos and Faux Pas to Avoid in Korean Dating Culture

Korean dating culture is unique and has its own set of cultural norms and expectations. While it may be exciting to learn about and experience a new culture, it is important to be aware of taboos and faux pas that may be offensive or disrespectful. In this chapter, we will explore taboos and faux pas to avoid in Korean dating culture, to help readers navigate the dating scene with cultural sensitivity and respect.

1. Making Physical Contact Too Soon

Physical contact is an important part of any romantic relationship, but in Korean dating culture, it is important to take things slow and build trust and respect before becoming physically intimate. Making physical contact too soon, such as trying to kiss or touch your partner on the first date, may be seen as disrespectful or inappropriate.

2. Ignoring Gender Roles and Expectations

Korean dating culture places a strong emphasis on traditional gender roles and expectations, and it is important to be aware of and respectful of these roles. For example, men are generally expected to take the lead in initiating and pursuing a relationship, and women are expected to be respectful and modest in their behavior and dress. Ignoring or disregarding these gender roles and expectations may be seen as disrespectful or offensive.

3. Disrespecting Elders or Authority Figures

Respect for elders and authority figures is a key value in Korean culture, and it is important to be respectful and deferential to these individuals. This can include showing respect for your partner's parents or grandparents, as well as being respectful to teachers, bosses, and other authority figures. Disrespecting elders or authority figures may be seen as disrespectful and offensive.

4. Being Too Loud or Expressive in Public

Korean culture places a strong emphasis on modesty and maintaining personal boundaries, and being too loud or expressive in public may be seen as disrespectful or inappropriate. It is important to be mindful of your behavior and to avoid making a scene in public settings.

5. Disrespecting Cultural and Historical Sites

Korea has a rich cultural and historical heritage, and it is important to be respectful of these sites and artifacts. Disrespecting cultural or historical sites, such as by taking inappropriate photos or making disrespectful comments, may be seen as disrespectful and offensive.

Korean dating culture has its own set of cultural norms and expectations, and it is important to be aware of and respectful of these norms when dating Korean men. By avoiding taboos and faux pas, readers can navigate the dating scene with cultural sensitivity and respect, and build strong and meaningful relationships with the Korean men they meet. By being respectful of traditional gender roles and expectations, elders and authority figures, and cultural and historical sites, readers can show their respect for Korean culture and build a deeper appreciation for this unique and fascinating country.

Communication and Language Barriers

Differences in Communication Styles and Expectations

Effective communication is essential for building strong and successful relationships, but communication styles and expectations can differ significantly between cultures. In Korean dating culture, communication styles and expectations may be different from what readers are used to in the West. In this chapter, we will explore the differences in communication styles and expectations between Korean dating culture and Western dating culture, to help readers better understand and appreciate these differences.

1. Indirect Communication

In Korean dating culture, indirect communication is often used to express feelings and opinions. This can involve using nonverbal cues, such as facial expressions or body language, to convey emotions. Direct communication is often seen as confrontational or aggressive, and is generally avoided in favor of more indirect forms of communication.

2. Respectful Language

Respectful language is an important part of Korean communication culture. Korean has a complex system of honorifics and polite language, which is used to show respect to elders, authority figures, and others in positions of power or seniority. It is important to be aware of and use appropriate respectful language when communicating with Korean men, especially in formal settings.

3. Group Orientation

Korean communication culture tends to be more group-oriented than individual-oriented. This means that Korean men may be more focused on the needs and expectations of their family or social group, rather than their individual desires or preferences. This can affect communication styles and expectations, as Korean men may prioritize group harmony over individual expression.

4. Nonverbal Cues

Nonverbal communication is an important part of Korean communication culture, and can include gestures, facial expressions, and body language. Understanding and interpreting these nonverbal cues is an important part of effective communication with Korean men.

5. Silence

Silence is often used as a form of communication in Korean dating culture. This can involve pauses in conversation, or long periods of reflection before responding to a question or comment. Silence is generally seen as a sign of respect and thoughtfulness, rather than awkwardness or discomfort.

Understanding and appreciating these differences is essential for building strong and successful relationships with Korean men. By being aware of indirect communication, using appropriate respectful language, being mindful of group orientation, interpreting nonverbal cues, and understanding the use of silence, readers can navigate the communication culture with cultural sensitivity and build meaningful connections with the Korean men they meet.

Common Challenges Faced by Non-Korean Speakers

For non-Korean speakers, navigating Korean dating culture can be challenging. Language barriers can make communication difficult, and cultural differences may be difficult to navigate without a basic understanding of Korean language and culture. In this chapter, we will explore common challenges faced by non-Korean speakers in Korean dating culture, and provide tips for overcoming these challenges and building strong and meaningful relationships.

1. Language Barriers

Language barriers are a common challenge faced by non-Korean speakers in Korean dating culture. Korean is a complex language with its own unique grammar and pronunciation, which can make it difficult for non-Korean speakers to understand and communicate effectively. It is important to be patient and understanding when communicating with Korean men, and to take steps to improve language skills, such as taking language classes or using language learning apps.

2. Cultural Differences

Cultural differences can also be a challenge for non-Korean speakers. Korean dating culture has its own unique set of social norms and expectations, which may be different from what non-Korean speakers are used to in their own culture. It is important to be aware of and respectful of these cultural differences, and to take steps to learn about Korean culture and customs.

3. Misunderstandings

Misunderstandings can arise in Korean dating culture due to language and cultural differences. It is important to clarify any misunderstandings as soon as they arise, and to be open and honest in communication. It is also important to be aware of cultural differences in communication styles and expectations, and to take steps to adapt to these differences.

4. Feeling Out of Place

Non-Korean speakers may also feel out of place in Korean dating culture, particularly if they are new to the culture or have limited experience with Korean language and customs. It is important to take steps to integrate into Korean culture, such as attending cultural events, trying Korean cuisine, and making an effort to meet and connect with Korean people.

5. Navigating Family and Social Expectations

Family and social expectations can be a challenge for non-Korean speakers in Korean dating culture. Korean culture places a strong emphasis on family and social relationships, and it is important to be aware of and respectful of these expectations. It is also important to communicate openly and honestly with family and social networks, and to be mindful of cultural differences in family and social dynamics.

Navigating Korean dating culture as a non-Korean speaker can be challenging, but with the right approach and understanding of cultural norms and expectations, it is possible to build strong and meaningful relationships with Korean men. By being patient and understanding with language barriers, learning about and respecting cultural differences, clarifying misunderstandings, integrating into Korean culture, and navigating family and social expectations, non-Korean speakers can navigate the dating scene with cultural sensitivity and build meaningful connections with the Korean men they meet.

Tips for Effective Communication and Building Trust

Effective communication and trust are essential for building strong and successful relationships with Korean men. However, communication styles and expectations can differ significantly between cultures, and building trust may require extra effort and understanding. In this chapter, we will explore tips for effective communication and building trust in Korean dating culture, to help readers navigate the dating scene with cultural sensitivity and respect.

1. Be Patient and Understanding

Effective communication and building trust in Korean dating culture may take more time and effort than in Western dating culture. It is important to be patient and understanding, and to take the time to build trust and rapport with Korean men. This may involve taking the time to learn about Korean culture and customs, and to be respectful of cultural differences in communication styles and expectations.

2. Use Clear and Respectful Language

Using clear and respectful language is an important part of effective communication in Korean dating culture. It is important to be mindful of respectful language and honorifics, and to use language that is clear and easy to understand. Using polite and respectful language can help to build trust and respect with Korean men.

3. Clarify Misunderstandings

Misunderstandings can arise in any relationship, but it is important to clarify these misunderstandings as soon as they arise. It is important to be open and honest in communication, and to seek clarification when necessary. This can help to build trust and understanding in the relationship.

4. Use Nonverbal Cues

Nonverbal cues are an important part of effective communication in Korean dating culture. This can include using facial expressions, body language, and tone of voice to convey emotions and feelings. Understanding and using nonverbal cues effectively can help to build trust and understanding with Korean men.

5. Show Respect and Empathy

Showing respect and empathy is an important part of building trust in Korean dating culture. It is important to be respectful of cultural norms and expectations, and to show empathy for the experiences and perspectives of Korean men. This can involve listening actively, showing interest in Korean culture and customs, and being respectful of individual needs and preferences.

Effective communication and building trust are essential for building strong and successful relationships with Korean men. By being patient and understanding, using clear and respectful language, clarifying misunderstandings, using nonverbal cues effectively, and showing respect and empathy, readers can navigate the dating scene with cultural sensitivity and build meaningful connections with the Korean men they meet. By taking the time to build trust and rapport, readers can develop long-lasting and fulfilling relationships with Korean men.

Korean Men's Personality Traits

Common Personality Traits of Korean Men

Korean men are known for their unique personalities and cultural values. Understanding these personality traits can help readers better understand and appreciate Korean dating culture. In this chapter, we will explore common personality traits of Korean men, to help readers build stronger and more meaningful relationships.

1. Respectful

Respect is a key value in Korean culture, and Korean men are known for their respectful behavior and language. They show respect for elders, authority figures, and others in positions of power or seniority. Korean men also show respect to their partners, and value open and honest communication.

2. Hardworking

Korean men are known for their strong work ethic and dedication to their careers. They often work long hours and prioritize their work over other aspects of their lives. This can make it challenging to balance work and relationships, but also demonstrates their commitment and dedication to achieving their goals.

3. Family-Oriented

Family is a key value in Korean culture, and Korean men are often very close to their families. They may prioritize family events and responsibilities over social or romantic commitments, and may seek partners who share their family values.

4. Modest

Modesty is an important value in Korean culture, and Korean men may be more reserved or modest in their behavior and dress. They may be less likely to engage in public displays of affection or boastful behavior.

5. Confident

Despite their modest behavior, Korean men can also be very confident in their abilities and achievements. They may have high expectations for themselves and their partners, and may seek partners who share their confidence and ambition.

6. Patriotic

Patriotism is a strong value in Korean culture, and Korean men are often proud of their country and its cultural heritage. They may value partners who appreciate and respect Korean culture, and who share their love of their homeland.

7. Romantic

Despite cultural differences in dating and relationships, Korean men can also be very romantic and affectionate. They may express their feelings through thoughtful gestures, such as surprise dates or small gifts, and may prioritize building emotional connections with their partners.

By understanding and appreciating these traits, readers can build stronger and more meaningful relationships with Korean men. By valuing respect, hard work, family, modesty, confidence, patriotism, and romance, readers can develop long-lasting and fulfilling relationships with Korean men, and gain a deeper appreciation for Korean culture and customs.

How Korean Men Differ from Western Men

Korean men have a unique set of cultural values and personality traits that differentiate them from Western men. Understanding these differences can help readers better appreciate Korean dating culture, and navigate cultural differences in relationships. In this chapter, we will explore some of the ways in which Korean men differ from Western men, to help readers build stronger and more meaningful relationships.

1. Cultural Values

Korean culture places a strong emphasis on respect, family, and social harmony, which can differ from the individualistic values emphasized in Western culture. Korean men may prioritize the needs and expectations of their family or social group, over their individual desires or preferences. This can affect communication styles, decision-making, and relationships with partners.

2. Communication Styles

Communication styles and expectations can also differ between Korean men and Western men. Korean communication culture tends to be more indirect and group-oriented, with a strong emphasis on nonverbal cues and respect for authority. Western communication culture tends to be more direct and individualistic, with a stronger emphasis on verbal expression and assertiveness.

3. Relationship Dynamics

Relationship dynamics can also differ between Korean men and Western men. Korean dating culture places a strong emphasis on building emotional connections and trust, and may involve more formal dating practices and social expectations. Western dating culture can be more casual and informal, and may involve a greater emphasis on physical attraction and sexual chemistry.

4. Personal Appearance

Korean men may also differ from Western men in their personal appearance and grooming habits. Korean men may place a greater emphasis on fashion and grooming, with a focus on clean and polished looks. Western men may place a greater emphasis on casual and comfortable styles.

5. Work-Life Balance

Korean men may also differ from Western men in their approach to work-life balance. Korean culture places a strong emphasis on hard work and dedication to one's career, which can make it challenging to balance work and relationships. Western culture places a greater emphasis on work-life balance, and may prioritize personal relationships over career success.

Korean men and Western men have unique sets of cultural values and personality traits that differentiate them from one another. By understanding and appreciating these differences, readers can navigate cultural differences in relationships and build stronger and more meaningful connections with Korean men. By being aware of differences in cultural values, communication styles, relationship dynamics, personal appearance, and work-life balance, readers can develop a deeper understanding of Korean dating culture and build fulfilling relationships with Korean men.

Cultural and Social Factors that Influence Korean Men's Behavior

Korean culture has a complex set of cultural and social factors that influence the behavior and attitudes of Korean men. Understanding these factors can help readers better appreciate Korean dating culture and build stronger and more meaningful relationships with Korean men. In this chapter, we will explore some of the cultural and social factors that influence Korean men's behavior.

1. Confucianism

Confucianism is a philosophical and ethical system that has had a profound influence on Korean culture. Confucianism emphasizes respect for authority, loyalty to family, and social harmony, which can influence Korean men's behavior and attitudes towards relationships.

2. Family Values

Family is a key value in Korean culture, and Korean men often have close relationships with their families. This can influence their behavior and attitudes towards relationships, as they may prioritize family obligations and expectations over individual desires.

3. Gender Roles

Gender roles and expectations can also influence Korean men's behavior. Traditional gender roles emphasize men's responsibility as breadwinners and women's responsibility for the home and family. However, attitudes towards gender roles are evolving in Korea, and many Korean men are increasingly open to more egalitarian relationships.

4. Social Pressure

Social pressure can also influence Korean men's behavior and attitudes towards relationships. Social norms and expectations in Korea can be quite strong, and Korean men may feel pressure to conform to these expectations. This can make it challenging to break away from traditional dating practices or social expectations.

5. Economic Factors

Economic factors can also influence Korean men's behavior and attitudes towards relationships. The high cost of living in Korea, combined with a competitive job market, can make it challenging for Korean men to balance career success with personal relationships. Economic factors may also influence decisions about marriage and starting a family.

Korean culture has a complex set of cultural and social factors that influence the behavior and attitudes of Korean men. By understanding and appreciating these factors, readers can develop a deeper understanding of Korean dating culture and build stronger and more meaningful relationships with Korean men. By being aware of the influence of Confucianism, family values, gender roles, social pressure, and economic factors, readers can navigate cultural differences in relationships and build fulfilling connections with Korean men.

The Korean Men's Appearance and Style

General Physical Traits and Clothing Styles of Korean Men

Physical appearance and style are important aspects of Korean culture, and they play a significant role in how Korean men are perceived by others. In this chapter, we will explore the general physical traits and clothing styles of Korean men, to help readers understand and appreciate their unique sense of fashion and aesthetics.

Physical Traits of Korean Men

Korean men are known for their distinct physical features, which include straight, jet-black hair, almond-shaped eyes, and smooth, clear skin. These physical traits are often considered desirable in Korean culture, and many Korean men take great care to maintain their appearance through grooming, skincare, and fashion.

In addition to these general features, there are also certain physical traits that are specific to Korean men. For example, many Korean men have a slim, lean physique, with broad shoulders and narrow hips. This body type is often attributed to the traditional Korean diet, which is rich in vegetables, rice, and lean protein.

Korean men also tend to have a unique facial structure, characterized by a prominent forehead, high cheekbones, and a V-shaped jawline. This facial structure is often considered attractive in Korean culture, and many Korean men use makeup and skincare products to enhance these features.

Clothing Styles of Korean Men

Korean men are known for their distinct sense of style, which is characterized by a combination of traditional and modern elements. Traditional Korean clothing, such as the hanbok, is often worn for formal occasions, while modern clothing styles are more commonly worn in everyday life.

One popular modern clothing style among Korean men is the "Korean streetwear" look, which features oversized clothing, bold prints, and bright colors. This style is often associated with the hip-hop and K-pop cultures, which have a significant influence on Korean fashion.

Korean men also tend to place a strong emphasis on grooming and accessories, such as hats, sunglasses, and watches. Many Korean men also wear jewelry, such as earrings and bracelets, which are considered fashionable and trendy.

The physical traits and clothing styles of Korean men are a reflection of their unique cultural identity and sense of aesthetics. From their straight black hair and almond-shaped eyes to their slim physique and distinctive facial structure, Korean men have a look that is both distinct and attractive. Their sense of style, which blends traditional and modern elements, is also a reflection of their cultural heritage and globalized outlook. By appreciating and understanding these physical traits and clothing styles, readers can gain a deeper appreciation for Korean culture and better connect with the Korean men they meet.

Common Hairstyles and Grooming Habits of Korean Men

Korean men are known for their stylish and meticulous grooming habits, which have helped to shape their unique sense of fashion and identity. From their hairstyles to their skincare routines, Korean men take great care in their appearance. In this chapter, we will explore the common hairstyles and grooming habits of Korean men, to help readers understand and appreciate their beauty rituals.

Hairstyles

Korean men have a wide variety of hairstyles to choose from, ranging from traditional to modern, and everything in between. Here are some of the most common hairstyles for Korean men:

1. Two-Block Cut: This hairstyle features short hair on the sides and back, with longer hair on top, creating a distinct two-block shape.
2. Side-Parted Hair: This classic hairstyle is characterized by a deep side part and slicked-back hair.
3. Undercut: This edgy hairstyle features shaved sides and longer hair on top, creating a dramatic contrast.
4. Slicked-Back Hair: This hairstyle is similar to the side-parted style, but with the hair slicked back instead of to the side.

5. Perm: This hairstyle involves using chemicals to create curls or waves in the hair, creating a unique texture and shape.

Grooming Habits

Korean men are known for their meticulous grooming habits, which include skincare, makeup, and haircare. Here are some of the most common grooming habits among Korean men:

1. Skincare: Korean men place a strong emphasis on skincare, using a variety of products such as toners, essences, and moisturizers to keep their skin clear and smooth.
2. Makeup: Many Korean men also use makeup to enhance their features and create a more polished look. This includes products such as BB cream, eyebrow pencils, and lip balm.
3. Haircare: Korean men take great care in their hair, using a variety of products such as hair gel, wax, and spray to create the perfect hairstyle.
4. Shaving: Korean men also place a strong emphasis on shaving, with many using traditional shaving tools such as straight razors or safety razors.
5. Nail Care: Some Korean men also place a strong emphasis on nail care, with many getting regular manicures to keep their nails looking clean and well-maintained.

The hairstyles and grooming habits of Korean men are a reflection of their unique sense of style and beauty. From their meticulous skincare routines to their trendy hairstyles, Korean men take great care in their appearance, and this has helped to shape their cultural identity.

Family and Social Expectations

Importance of Family and Social Networks in Korean Culture

Family and social networks are of great importance in Korean culture. Korean men often have close relationships with their families and social circles, which can influence their behavior and attitudes towards relationships. Understanding the importance of family and social networks in Korean culture can help readers navigate cultural differences in relationships and build stronger and more meaningful connections with Korean men. In this chapter, we will explore the importance of family and social networks in Korean culture.

1. Familial Relationships

Family is a key value in Korean culture, and Korean men often have close relationships with their families. Familial relationships are based on respect, loyalty, and obligation. Korean men may prioritize family events and responsibilities over social or romantic commitments, and may seek partners who share their family values.

2. Social Circles

Social networks are also important in Korean culture. Social circles are often formed through school, work, or common interests, and can be a source of support and identity. Korean men may place a great emphasis on maintaining their social networks, and may expect their partners to become a part of these networks.

3. Group Mentality

Korean culture places a strong emphasis on group mentality and social harmony. This can influence Korean men's behavior and attitudes towards relationships, as they may prioritize the needs and expectations of their social group over their individual desires. This can affect communication styles, decision-making, and relationships with partners.

4. Social Pressure

Social pressure can also influence Korean men's behavior and attitudes towards relationships. Social norms and expectations in Korea can be quite strong, and Korean men may feel pressure to conform to these expectations. This can make it challenging to break away from traditional dating practices or social expectations.

5. Importance of Marriage and Family

Marriage and family are important values in Korean culture. Korean men may prioritize finding a partner for marriage and starting a family. This can influence their behavior and attitudes towards relationships, as they may seek partners who share their values and are open to building long-lasting connections.

Family and social networks are of great importance in Korean culture. By understanding and appreciating the importance of familial relationships, social networks, group mentality, social pressure, and the importance of marriage and family, readers can navigate cultural differences in relationships and build stronger and more meaningful connections with Korean men. By being respectful of family and social values, and by understanding the influence of group mentality and social pressure, readers can develop fulfilling relationships with Korean men, and gain a deeper appreciation for Korean culture and customs.

Expectations and Pressures on Men to Fulfill Certain Roles in Korean Culture

Korean culture places a strong emphasis on social norms and expectations, which can put pressure on Korean men to fulfill certain roles and expectations. These expectations can influence Korean men's behavior and attitudes towards relationships, and can create challenges in building strong and fulfilling connections. In this chapter, we will explore the expectations and pressures on men to fulfill certain roles in Korean culture.

1. Breadwinner

Traditionally, Korean men are expected to be the primary breadwinners in their families. This can create pressure to prioritize work and career over personal relationships, and can make it challenging to balance work and family obligations. Korean men may also feel pressure to maintain a certain level of income or status in their careers.

2. Patriarch

Korean culture places a strong emphasis on hierarchical relationships, and Korean men may be expected to assume the role of patriarch within their families or social groups. This can create pressure to be authoritative and make important decisions, which can affect relationships with partners and other family members.

3. Filial Piety

Filial piety, or respect for one's elders, is a key value in Korean culture. Korean men may feel pressure to prioritize the needs and expectations of their parents or older family members over their individual desires. This can affect decision-making in relationships and can create challenges in building strong emotional connections.

4. Social Expectations

Social expectations can also create pressure on Korean men to fulfill certain roles and expectations. Korean culture places a strong emphasis on group mentality and social harmony, which can influence behavior and attitudes towards relationships. Korean men may feel pressure to conform to social norms and expectations, which can create challenges in expressing their individual desires and needs.

5. Masculine Norms

Masculine norms and expectations can also influence Korean men's behavior and attitudes towards relationships. Korean culture places a strong emphasis on traditional gender roles, which can create pressure for Korean men to be assertive, dominant, and independent. This can affect communication styles and emotional expression, which can create challenges in building strong emotional connections with partners.

Navigating and Respecting Expectations as a Partner in Korean Culture

Navigating cultural expectations in a relationship with a Korean man can be challenging, but it is important to understand and respect these expectations to build strong and fulfilling connections. In this chapter, we will explore some strategies for navigating and respecting expectations as a partner in Korean culture.

1. Communication

Communication is key to navigating and respecting expectations in a relationship with a Korean man. It is important to have open and honest conversations about expectations, cultural differences, and individual desires. Active listening, nonverbal cues, and respect for authority can also help facilitate effective communication.

2. Respect for Family

Respect for family is a key value in Korean culture, and it is important to show respect and appreciation for your partner's family. This may involve participating in family events, acknowledging their expectations and needs, and showing gratitude for their support.

3. Understanding Gender Roles

Understanding gender roles and expectations in Korean culture can help partners navigate expectations and build stronger connections. It is important to acknowledge and respect traditional gender roles, but also to be open to evolving attitudes towards gender and individual expression.

4. Building Social Connections

Building social connections with your partner's friends and social network can also help navigate and respect cultural expectations. Participating in social events, showing interest in common interests, and respecting group mentality can help partners build stronger and more meaningful connections.

5. Balancing Work and Relationships

Balancing work and relationships can be a challenge in Korean culture, but it is important to acknowledge and respect your partner's career goals and obligations. Finding a balance between personal and professional life, supporting your partner's career goals, and being flexible in scheduling can help partners navigate expectations and build stronger emotional connections.

Navigating and respecting cultural expectations in a relationship with a Korean man requires patience, empathy, and understanding. By practicing effective communication, showing respect for family, understanding gender roles, building social connections, and balancing work and relationships, partners can navigate cultural differences and build strong and fulfilling connections with Korean men. By respecting and appreciating Korean culture and customs, readers can develop a deeper understanding of Korean dating culture, and build fulfilling relationships with Korean men.

Intimacy and Physical Touch

Attitudes Towards Intimacy and Physical Touch in Korean Culture

Attitudes towards intimacy and physical touch can vary widely across cultures, and it is important to understand and respect these attitudes to build strong and fulfilling relationships. In Korean culture, attitudes towards intimacy and physical touch are influenced by a variety of factors, including traditional gender roles, Confucianism, and social expectations. In this chapter, we will explore the attitudes towards intimacy and physical touch in Korean culture.

1. Traditional Gender Roles

Traditional gender roles in Korean culture emphasize the importance of modesty and restraint in women's behavior, which can affect attitudes towards intimacy and physical touch. Korean men may expect women to be reserved in their behavior and physical expressions of affection, which can make it challenging to initiate physical contact or express intimacy.

2. Confucianism

Confucianism places a strong emphasis on respect for authority and social harmony, which can influence attitudes towards intimacy and physical touch. In Korean culture, physical contact may be seen as a private and intimate act that should be reserved for close relationships, such as marriage or long-term partnerships.

3. Social Expectations

Social expectations and norms can also influence attitudes towards intimacy and physical touch in Korean culture. Public displays of affection may be frowned upon, and Korean couples may be expected to maintain a certain level of decorum in their behavior and expressions of affection.

4. Western Influence

Attitudes towards intimacy and physical touch are evolving in Korea, and Western influence may be contributing to a more open and accepting attitude towards physical contact and expressions of affection. However, these changes are still relatively recent and may not be accepted or embraced by all segments of Korean society.

5. Building Emotional Connections

Building emotional connections and trust is key to developing intimacy and physical touch in Korean relationships. It is important to respect your partner's comfort level and communicate openly about physical boundaries and desires. Building emotional connections can also help partners feel more comfortable expressing physical affection and intimacy.

How to Initiate and Build Physical Intimacy with a Korean Man

Initiating and building physical intimacy with a Korean man can be challenging, as attitudes towards physical touch and intimacy can vary widely across cultures. However, by understanding cultural expectations and practicing effective communication, partners can navigate these challenges and build strong and fulfilling relationships. In this chapter, we will explore some strategies for initiating and building physical intimacy with a Korean man.

1. Communication

Effective communication is key to building physical intimacy in a relationship with a Korean man. It is important to have open and honest conversations about physical boundaries, desires, and expectations. Respectful and non-judgmental communication can help partners understand and respect each other's comfort levels and desires.

2. Building Emotional Connections

Building emotional connections is essential to developing physical intimacy in Korean relationships. By sharing experiences, interests, and personal stories, partners can build trust and emotional connections that pave the way for physical intimacy.

3. Respect for Boundaries

Respect for boundaries is critical to building physical intimacy in a relationship with a Korean man. It is important to respect your partner's comfort level and desires, and to communicate openly and honestly about physical boundaries.

Respecting boundaries helps partners build trust and emotional connections, and creates a foundation for developing physical intimacy.

4. Gradual Progression

Building physical intimacy in a relationship with a Korean man may require a gradual progression, as attitudes towards physical touch and intimacy may be more reserved or traditional. It is important to respect your partner's pace and comfort level, and to allow physical intimacy to develop naturally over time.

5. Non-Verbal Cues

Non-verbal cues can also be helpful in initiating and building physical intimacy with a Korean man. Small gestures, such as holding hands or leaning in for a hug, can communicate intimacy and affection without words. Paying attention to your partner's non-verbal cues can also help you understand their comfort level and desires.

Initiating and building physical intimacy with a Korean man requires patience, empathy, and understanding. By practicing effective communication, building emotional connections, respecting physical boundaries, allowing for a gradual progression, and paying attention to non-verbal cues, partners can navigate cultural differences and build strong and fulfilling physical connections with Korean men. By understanding and respecting cultural attitudes towards physical touch and intimacy, readers can develop a deeper appreciation for Korean culture and customs, and build fulfilling relationships with Korean men.

Korean Attitudes Towards Sex and Sexuality

Attitudes towards sex and sexuality vary widely across cultures, and it is important to understand and respect these attitudes to build strong and fulfilling relationships. In Korean culture, attitudes towards sex and sexuality are influenced by a variety of factors, including traditional gender roles, social expectations, and Confucianism. In this chapter, we will explore some strategies for understanding Korean attitudes towards sex and sexuality.

1. Traditional Gender Roles

Traditional gender roles in Korean culture can affect attitudes towards sex and sexuality. Women may be expected to be more reserved and modest in their behavior, while men may be expected to take the lead in initiating physical intimacy. However, attitudes towards gender roles are evolving in Korea, and it is important to acknowledge and respect individual expressions of sexuality and desire.

2. Social Expectations

Social expectations and norms can also influence attitudes towards sex and sexuality in Korean culture. Korean couples may be expected to maintain a certain level of decorum in their behavior and expressions of affection, which can create challenges in exploring sexual desires and needs.

3. Confucianism

Confucianism places a strong emphasis on social harmony and respect for authority, which can affect attitudes towards sex and sexuality. Sexual expression may be seen as a private and intimate act that should be reserved for close relationships, such as marriage or long-term partnerships.

4.   Western Influence

Western influence may be contributing to a more open and accepting attitude towards sex and sexuality in Korea, but these attitudes are still evolving and may not be embraced by all segments of Korean society.

5.   Building Trust and Communication

Building trust and effective communication are key to exploring and understanding attitudes towards sex and sexuality in Korean relationships. Partners can practice active listening, non-judgmental attitudes, and respect for boundaries and comfort levels to create a safe and comfortable environment for exploring sexual desires and needs.

Marriage and Long-term Relationships

Attitudes and Expectations Towards Marriage and Commitment in Korean Culture

Attitudes and expectations towards marriage and commitment can vary widely across cultures, and it is important to understand and respect these attitudes to build strong and fulfilling relationships. In Korean culture, attitudes towards marriage and commitment are influenced by a variety of factors, including traditional gender roles, family values, and Confucianism. In this chapter, we will explore some strategies for understanding attitudes and expectations towards marriage and commitment in Korean culture.

1. Traditional Gender Roles

Traditional gender roles in Korean culture can affect attitudes towards marriage and commitment. Women may be expected to prioritize marriage and family over career and personal goals, while men may be expected to provide for and protect their families. However, attitudes towards gender roles are evolving in Korea, and it is important to acknowledge and respect individual expressions of marriage and commitment.

2. Family Values

Family values are important considerations in Korean attitudes towards marriage and commitment. Korean families may prioritize the needs of the family unit over individual desires and goals, and marriage may be seen as a way to strengthen family ties and continue family legacies. It is also common for Korean couples to seek the approval of their families before making major decisions around marriage and commitment.

3. Confucianism

Confucianism places a strong emphasis on social harmony and respect for authority, which can affect attitudes towards marriage and commitment. Marriage may be seen as a way to maintain social order and stability, and commitment to one's partner may be seen as a way to fulfill one's social obligations.

4. Modern Attitudes Towards Marriage and Commitment

Modern attitudes towards marriage and commitment are evolving in Korea, and some individuals may prioritize personal goals and desires over traditional family and social expectations. It is also becoming more common for individuals to seek out romantic relationships based on shared interests and values, rather than solely on familial connections or economic considerations.

5. Building Strong and Fulfilling Relationships

Building strong and fulfilling relationships requires mutual respect, effective communication, and a shared commitment to personal and relationship goals. Partners can practice active listening, respect for boundaries and comfort levels, and non-judgmental attitudes to create a safe and comfortable environment for exploring attitudes towards marriage and commitment. It is also important to communicate openly and honestly about personal goals and desires, and to work together to build a shared vision for the future.

Traditional Gender Roles and Expectations in Korean Marriages

Traditional gender roles and expectations can have a significant impact on relationships, particularly in the context of marriage. In this chapter, we will explore some strategies for understanding and navigating traditional gender roles and expectations in Korean marriages.

1. Gender Roles in Korean Marriages

Traditional gender roles in Korean marriages are deeply ingrained in Korean culture. Men are often expected to be the breadwinners and provide for the family, while women are expected to manage the household and care for children. These gender roles are often reinforced through social expectations, including family pressures and media representations.

2. Confucianism and Marriage

Confucianism places a strong emphasis on social order and respect for authority, which can influence attitudes towards gender roles and expectations in Korean marriages. Confucian values prioritize the needs of the family and the community over individual desires, and the role of the wife in a marriage is often seen as one of support for her husband and his family.

3. Family Values and Marriage

Family values play a significant role in Korean marriages, and the family unit is often prioritized over individual needs and desires. Korean couples may seek the approval and support of their families before making major decisions around marriage, and family dynamics can play a significant role in shaping the gender roles and expectations within a marriage.

4. Navigating Traditional Gender Roles and Expectations

Navigating traditional gender roles and expectations in Korean marriages can be challenging, particularly for those who do not adhere to traditional gender norms. Partners can practice effective communication, mutual respect, and a willingness to compromise to create a more equitable and fulfilling marriage. It is also important to acknowledge and address individual desires and goals, and to work together to build a shared vision for the future.

5. Modern Attitudes towards Gender Roles and Expectations

Modern attitudes towards gender roles and expectations in Korean marriages are evolving, particularly among younger generations. Women are increasingly seeking greater autonomy and independence, and men are becoming more involved in domestic responsibilities. While traditional gender roles and expectations are still prevalent in Korean marriages, there is also growing recognition of the importance of mutual respect and partnership in building strong and fulfilling relationships.

Family Dynamics and In-Laws

Role of Family and In-Laws in Korean Relationships

Family and in-laws play a significant role in Korean culture, and this can have a significant impact on relationships. In a relationship with a Korean man, partners may need to navigate the expectations and pressures of their partner's family, and find ways to build strong relationships with their in-laws. In this chapter, we will explore the role of family and in-laws in Korean relationships, and strategies for navigating these relationships.

1. Family Expectations and Pressures

Family expectations and pressures can play a significant role in Korean relationships. Korean families may prioritize the needs of the family unit over individual desires and goals, and partners may need to seek the approval and support of their partner's family before making major decisions around marriage and commitment. Partners may also need to navigate traditional gender roles and expectations within their partner's family.

2. Building Strong Relationships with In-Laws

Building strong relationships with in-laws is critical for navigating the expectations and pressures of Korean families. Partners can practice respect, patience, and empathy when interacting with their partner's family, and seek out opportunities to build common interests and experiences. It is also important to communicate openly and honestly with in-laws, and to work together to find ways to build strong relationships based on mutual respect and understanding.

3. Navigating Conflicts with In-Laws

Conflicts with in-laws can be challenging for Korean relationships, particularly when there are cultural differences and language barriers. Partners can practice effective communication, respect for boundaries and comfort levels, and non-judgmental attitudes to create a safe and comfortable environment for navigating conflicts. It is also important to seek out support from trusted family members and friends, and to work together to find solutions that honor and respect each other's values and needs.

4. Finding Common Ground with Family

Finding common ground with family is important for building strong relationships with in-laws and navigating the expectations and pressures of Korean families. Partners can seek out opportunities to engage with their partner's family around common interests and values, and to explore cultural events and festivals together. It is also important to acknowledge and respect individual preferences and needs around cultural differences, and to find ways to celebrate important cultural events and traditions.

5. Building a Strong Partnership

Building a strong partnership is key to navigating the role of family and in-laws in Korean relationships. Partners can practice effective communication, mutual respect, and a shared commitment to personal and relationship goals. It is also important to communicate openly and honestly about personal desires and goals, and to work together to build a shared vision for the future that honors and respects both individual needs and family expectations.

The role of family and in-laws in Korean relationships can be complex and challenging, but it is possible to navigate these relationships with patience, empathy, and effective communication. By building strong relationships with in-laws, finding common ground with family, and building a strong partnership with their Korean partner, readers can build fulfilling and meaningful relationships with Korean men. By respecting and appreciating Korean culture and customs, readers can develop a deeper understanding of Korean dating culture and build strong and fulfilling relationships with Korean men.

Common Challenges Faced by Non-Korean Partners in Navigating Family Dynamics

Navigating family dynamics in a Korean relationship can be challenging, particularly for non-Korean partners who may not be familiar with Korean culture and traditions. Partners may need to navigate language barriers, differing attitudes towards family and gender roles, and social pressures to conform to cultural expectations. In this chapter, we will explore some of the common challenges faced by non-Korean partners in navigating family dynamics in Korean relationships, and strategies for addressing these challenges.

1. Language Barriers

Language barriers can be a significant challenge for non-Korean partners in navigating family dynamics. Partners may struggle to communicate effectively with their Korean partner's family, which can create misunderstandings and frustrations. It is important for partners to seek out language classes and practice effective communication strategies to build stronger relationships with their partner's family.

2. Differing Attitudes towards Family and Gender Roles

Differing attitudes towards family and gender roles can also pose challenges for non-Korean partners. Korean families may prioritize the needs of the family unit over individual desires and goals, and traditional gender roles may be reinforced through social expectations. Non-Korean partners may need to navigate these attitudes and find ways to build strong relationships with their partner's family, while also honoring their own values and beliefs.

3. Social Pressures to Conform to Cultural Expectations

Social pressures to conform to cultural expectations can also pose challenges for non-Korean partners. Korean families may have specific expectations around behavior, dress, and social norms, which can be difficult for non-Korean partners to navigate. It is important for partners to communicate openly and honestly with their partner's family, and to find ways to respectfully address any concerns or misunderstandings.

4. Navigating Conflicts with In-Laws

Conflicts with in-laws can be challenging for non-Korean partners, particularly when there are cultural differences and language barriers. It is important for partners to practice effective communication, respect for boundaries and comfort levels, and non-judgmental attitudes to create a safe and comfortable environment for navigating conflicts. It is also important to seek out support from trusted family members and friends, and to work together to find solutions that honor and respect each other's values and needs.

5. Finding Common Ground with Family

Finding common ground with family is important for building strong relationships with in-laws and navigating the expectations and pressures of Korean families. Partners can seek out opportunities to engage with their partner's family around common interests and values, and to explore cultural events and festivals together. It is also important to acknowledge and respect individual preferences and needs around cultural differences, and to find ways to celebrate important cultural events and traditions.

Finances and Money Matters

Attitudes towards Finances and Money in Korean Culture

Finances and money are important aspects of any relationship, and can be particularly significant in Korean culture. Attitudes towards finances and money in Korean culture can reflect traditional values around family and social status, and can impact how relationships are formed and sustained. In this chapter, we will explore attitudes towards finances and money in Korean culture, and strategies for navigating these attitudes in Korean relationships.

   1. Family Obligations

Family obligations are a significant aspect of Korean culture, and can impact attitudes towards finances and money. In Korean culture, it is common for adult children to financially support their parents and siblings, and to prioritize family needs over individual desires. Partners may need to navigate these expectations and find ways to honor their own financial goals and obligations while also meeting the needs of their family.

   2. Social Status and Image

Social status and image can also play a role in attitudes towards finances and money in Korean culture. In Korean culture, there may be pressure to maintain a certain image or status through material possessions or financial success. Partners may need to navigate these pressures and find ways to prioritize their own values and goals over external pressures.

3. Saving and Investing

Saving and investing are important aspects of Korean culture, and may be prioritized over spending and consumption. Partners may need to navigate these attitudes and find ways to balance their own financial goals with the expectations of their family and culture.

4. Education and Career

Education and career are highly valued in Korean culture, and may be prioritized over immediate financial gain. Partners may need to navigate these attitudes and find ways to balance their own financial goals with the expectations of their family and culture, while also pursuing their educational and career aspirations.

5. Personal Debt and Financial Responsibility

Personal debt and financial responsibility are also important aspects of Korean culture, and may be viewed as a reflection of personal character and responsibility. Partners may need to navigate these attitudes and find ways to address personal debt and financial responsibility in a way that honors their own values and goals.

Attitudes towards finances and money can play a significant role in Korean relationships, and may reflect traditional values around family and social status. By navigating family obligations, social status and image, saving and investing, education and career, personal debt and financial responsibility, partners can build strong and fulfilling relationships that honor their own financial goals and values, while also respecting the expectations and pressures of Korean culture.

Expectations and Norms for Financial Responsibility in Relationships

Financial responsibility is an important aspect of any relationship, and can be particularly significant in Korean culture. Expectations and norms for financial responsibility in relationships can reflect traditional values around family and social status, and can impact how relationships are formed and sustained. In this chapter, we will explore expectations and norms for financial responsibility in Korean relationships, and strategies for navigating these expectations in a way that honors personal values and goals.

1. Splitting Expenses

In Korean relationships, it is common for partners to split expenses evenly or for the person who makes more money to contribute more to expenses. Partners may need to navigate these expectations and find a system that works for their individual financial situation and values.

2. Gift Giving

Gift giving is an important aspect of Korean culture, and may be used as a way to express love and appreciation in relationships. Partners may need to navigate these expectations and find ways to express love and appreciation in a way that honors their own financial goals and values.

3. Family Obligations

Family obligations are a significant aspect of Korean culture, and may impact attitudes towards finances and money in relationships. Partners may need to navigate these expectations and find ways to balance their own financial goals and obligations with the needs of their family.

4. Communication and Transparency

Open communication and transparency are critical for navigating expectations and norms for financial responsibility in Korean relationships. Partners should be honest about their financial goals, needs, and limitations, and work together to find a system that honors both partners' values and goals.

5. Joint Financial Planning

Joint financial planning can be an effective way to navigate expectations and norms for financial responsibility in Korean relationships. Partners can work together to set shared financial goals, develop a budget, and make financial decisions together.

6. Personal Financial Responsibility

Personal financial responsibility is also an important aspect of Korean relationships. Partners should take responsibility for their own financial goals and obligations, and work together to find a system that honors both partners' values and goals.

How to Navigate Financial Differences and Build a Healthy Financial Future Together

Navigating financial differences and building a healthy financial future together is an important aspect of any relationship, and can be particularly challenging in Korean culture. Differences in values, goals, and obligations around finances can create tension and conflict in relationships. In this chapter, we will explore strategies for navigating financial differences and building a healthy financial future together in Korean relationships.

1. Identify and Discuss Differences

The first step in navigating financial differences is to identify and discuss them openly and honestly. Partners should take the time to understand each other's financial goals, values, and obligations, and work together to find a system that honors both partners' needs.

2. Establish Shared Financial Goals

Establishing shared financial goals is an effective way to navigate financial differences and build a healthy financial future together. Partners should work together to set specific and measurable goals, such as saving for a down payment on a home or paying off debt.

3. Develop a Budget

Developing a budget is another effective way to navigate financial differences and build a healthy financial future together. Partners should work together to create a realistic budget that reflects both partners' needs and priorities.

4. Consider Joint and Individual Accounts

Partners should consider whether to have joint and/or individual accounts. Joint accounts can be effective for shared expenses, while individual accounts can provide more independence and flexibility.

5. Plan for the Future

Planning for the future is an important aspect of building a healthy financial future together. Partners should discuss their long-term financial goals, such as retirement or children's education, and work together to develop a plan to achieve those goals.

6. Seek Professional Help

Seeking professional help, such as a financial planner or counselor, can be effective in navigating financial differences and building a healthy financial future together. Partners should be open to seeking outside help to address financial challenges and build a stronger relationship.

Navigating financial differences and building a healthy financial future together is an important aspect of any relationship, and can be particularly challenging in Korean culture. By identifying and discussing differences, establishing shared financial goals, developing a budget, considering joint and individual accounts, planning for the future, and seeking professional help, partners can build a strong and fulfilling relationship that honors both partners' financial goals and values. By respecting and appreciating Korean culture and customs, readers can develop a deeper understanding of Korean dating culture and build strong and fulfilling relationships with Korean men.

Living in Korea with a Korean Partner

Overview of Korean Culture and Daily Life

Korean culture is rich and diverse, with a long and complex history that has shaped modern Korean society. Understanding Korean culture and daily life is essential for building strong and fulfilling relationships with Korean men. In this chapter, we will explore the various aspects of Korean culture and daily life, including language, food, customs, and social norms.

1. Language

Korean is the official language of South Korea, and is spoken by over 75 million people worldwide. Understanding the Korean language and culture can be helpful in building relationships with Korean men, and can show a willingness to embrace and appreciate Korean culture.

2. Food

Food is an important aspect of Korean culture, with a wide variety of dishes and flavors that reflect the country's history and geography. Korean cuisine is known for its bold and spicy flavors, with popular dishes such as kimchi, bibimbap, and bulgogi. Sharing food and trying new dishes can be an effective way to connect with Korean men and show an appreciation for Korean culture.

3. Customs and Traditions

Customs and traditions are an important part of Korean culture, and reflect the country's long and complex history. Customs and traditions include bowing as a sign of respect, removing shoes before entering homes, and observing holidays such as Chuseok and Seollal. Understanding and respecting these customs can show a willingness to embrace Korean culture and build stronger relationships with Korean men.

4. Social Norms

Social norms in Korea can be different from those in Western countries, and understanding these norms is essential for building strong relationships with Korean men. Social norms include the importance of hierarchy and respect, the value placed on education and achievement, and the emphasis on family and community. Understanding and respecting these social norms can be effective in building stronger relationships with Korean men.

5. Entertainment and Leisure

Entertainment and leisure are important aspects of Korean daily life, with a wide variety of music, television shows, and sports that reflect the country's popular culture. Korean dramas and K-pop music have gained popularity around the world, and can be effective in building connections with Korean men who share these interests.

Tips for Adjusting to Life in Korea as a Foreign Partner

Adjusting to life in Korea as a foreign partner can be a challenging and rewarding experience. Navigating cultural differences, language barriers, and social norms can require patience, flexibility, and an open mind. In this chapter, we will explore strategies and tips for adjusting to life in Korea as a foreign partner, and building strong and fulfilling relationships with Korean men.

1. Learn the Language

Learning the Korean language is an effective way to adjust to life in Korea as a foreign partner. Learning Korean can improve communication with Korean partners and their families, and can show a willingness to embrace Korean culture.

2. Embrace Korean Food and Culture

Embracing Korean food and culture is an effective way to adjust to life in Korea as a foreign partner. Trying new foods, attending cultural events, and learning about Korean customs and traditions can show a willingness to embrace and appreciate Korean culture.

3. Seek Support and Community

Seeking support and community is an important aspect of adjusting to life in Korea as a foreign partner. Joining expat groups or seeking out local Korean communities can provide opportunities for socialization and support.

4. Be Open and Flexible

Being open and flexible is essential for adjusting to life in Korea as a foreign partner. Navigating cultural differences and social norms may require a willingness to adapt and learn, and a willingness to embrace new experiences.

5. Communicate with Your Partner

Open communication with your Korean partner is critical for adjusting to life in Korea as a foreign partner. Communicating about expectations, challenges, and needs can improve understanding and build stronger relationships.

6. Find Activities and Hobbies

Finding activities and hobbies that align with personal interests can be effective in adjusting to life in Korea as a foreign partner. Participating in local activities and hobbies can provide opportunities for socialization and building new connections.

Adjusting to life in Korea as a foreign partner can be a challenging and rewarding experience. By learning the language, embracing Korean food and culture, seeking support and community, being open and flexible, communicating with your partner, and finding activities and hobbies, foreign partners can navigate cultural differences and build strong and fulfilling relationships with Korean men. By respecting and appreciating Korean culture and customs, readers can embrace the rich and diverse culture of Korea and build strong and fulfilling relationships with Korean men.

Common Challenges and Strategies for Building a Successful Life Together

Building a successful life together with a Korean partner can be a challenging and rewarding experience. Navigating cultural differences, managing finances, and balancing personal and professional goals can require patience, compromise, and communication. In this chapter, we will explore common challenges and strategies for building a successful life together with a Korean partner.

1. Navigating Cultural Differences

Cultural differences can create challenges in relationships, but they can also provide opportunities for growth and learning. Partners should be open and respectful of each other's cultural backgrounds, and work together to find common ground and navigate cultural differences.

2. Managing Finances

Managing finances is an important aspect of building a successful life together. Partners should be transparent and honest about their financial situations, and work together to develop a budget and financial plan that reflects both partners' needs and goals.

3. Balancing Personal and Professional Goals

Balancing personal and professional goals can be challenging in relationships, particularly when partners have different priorities or career paths. Partners should be supportive of each other's goals and work together to find a balance that allows both partners to achieve their personal and professional aspirations.

4. Communication

Communication is critical for building a successful life together. Partners should be open and honest with each other, and communicate regularly about expectations, challenges, and needs. Effective communication can improve understanding and build stronger relationships.

5. Seeking Help

Seeking help, such as counseling or therapy, can be effective in overcoming challenges and building a successful life together. Partners should be open to seeking outside help to address challenges and build a stronger relationship.

6. Prioritizing Quality Time

Prioritizing quality time is essential for building a successful life together. Partners should make time for each other and find ways to strengthen their connection, such as by engaging in shared hobbies or taking regular vacations together.

Building a successful life together with a Korean partner can be a challenging and rewarding experience. By navigating cultural differences, managing finances, balancing personal and professional goals, communicating effectively, seeking help when needed, and prioritizing quality time, partners can build strong and fulfilling relationships that honor both partners' needs and goals. By respecting and appreciating Korean culture and customs, readers can develop a deeper understanding of Korean dating culture and build strong and fulfilling relationships with Korean men.

What Korean Men Find Attractive in Women

Physical and Personality Traits Valued by Korean Men

Physical and personality traits are important considerations for Korean men when looking for a partner. While individual preferences may vary, there are some common traits that are generally valued in Korean dating culture. In this chapter, we will explore physical and personality traits that are valued by Korean men.

1. Physical Traits

Physical appearance is an important consideration for Korean men when looking for a partner. While individual preferences may vary, there are some common physical traits that are generally valued in Korean dating culture, including:

- Fair Skin: Fair skin is often associated with beauty and femininity in Korean culture, and many Korean men prefer partners with fair skin.
- Slender Build: A slender build is often preferred in Korean dating culture, with a focus on a petite and feminine physique.
- Big Eyes: Big, expressive eyes are often considered attractive in Korean dating culture, and can convey a sense of innocence and vulnerability.
- Straight Hair: Straight, silky hair is often preferred in Korean dating culture, with a focus on well-maintained and healthy hair.

2. Personality Traits

Personality traits are also important considerations for Korean men when looking for a partner. While individual preferences may vary, there are some common personality traits that are generally valued in Korean dating culture, including:

- Respectfulness: Respectfulness is a key value in Korean culture, and is often valued in relationships. Partners who show respect towards their partner's family and cultural background are often preferred.
- Education and Intelligence: Education and intelligence are often valued in Korean dating culture, with a focus on partners who are well-educated and intellectually curious.
- Emotional Stability: Emotional stability is often valued in Korean dating culture, with a focus on partners who are emotionally mature and able to handle stress and challenges.
- Loyalty: Loyalty is a key value in Korean dating culture, with a focus on partners who are committed to their relationship and willing to work through challenges together.

Common Misconceptions and Stereotypes about Korean Men's Preferences

Korean dating culture can be complex and nuanced, and there are many misconceptions and stereotypes about Korean men's preferences. These stereotypes can perpetuate harmful myths and reinforce narrow beauty standards, and can create misunderstandings and miscommunications in relationships. In this chapter, we will explore common misconceptions and stereotypes about Korean men's preferences.

1. All Korean Men Prefer Fair Skin and Slender Builds

One common stereotype about Korean men's preferences is that they all prefer partners with fair skin and slender builds. While these traits are often valued in Korean dating culture, individual preferences can vary greatly, and there is no one "ideal" physical type.

2. Korean Men Only Date Korean Women

Another common misconception is that Korean men only date Korean women. While there may be cultural and language barriers that can make dating non-Korean partners more challenging, many Korean men are open to dating partners of different backgrounds and nationalities.

3. Korean Men are Overly Traditional and Patriarchal

Another stereotype about Korean men is that they are overly traditional and patriarchal, with rigid gender roles and expectations. While there may be some truth to this stereotype in some cases, it is not true for all Korean men. Many Korean men are open-minded and progressive, and are interested in building equal and respectful relationships with their partners.

4. Korean Men are Reserved and Emotionally Closed-Off

Another common stereotype about Korean men is that they are reserved and emotionally closed-off, with limited emotional expression or communication. While cultural differences can create communication challenges in relationships, it is not fair to assume that all Korean men are emotionally closed-off or unwilling to express their feelings.

5. Korean Men Only Value Intelligence and Education

Another stereotype about Korean men is that they only value partners who are highly educated and intelligent. While education and intelligence may be valued in Korean dating culture, there are many other important personality traits and values that Korean men look for in a partner, including loyalty, respectfulness, emotional stability, and more.

Misconceptions and stereotypes about Korean men's preferences can perpetuate harmful myths and create misunderstandings in relationships. While cultural differences and beauty standards may influence Korean men's preferences, individual preferences can vary greatly, and it is important to approach each relationship with an open mind and a willingness to communicate openly and honestly. By challenging these stereotypes and striving for deeper understanding and appreciation of Korean dating culture, readers can build stronger and more fulfilling relationships with Korean men.

How to Embrace Your Unique Qualities and Attract a Korean Man

Attracting a Korean man can be a rewarding and exciting experience, but it can also be challenging and intimidating, especially for those who are unfamiliar with Korean dating culture. However, by embracing your unique qualities and learning more about Korean dating culture, you can build a stronger and more fulfilling relationship with a Korean man. In this chapter, we will explore how to embrace your unique qualities and attract a Korean man.

1. Embrace Your Cultural Background

One of the best ways to attract a Korean man is to embrace your own cultural background. Many Korean men appreciate partners who are proud of their own culture and background, and are willing to share their own experiences and perspectives.

2. Focus on Your Personal Qualities and Values

While physical appearance can be important, focusing solely on your looks may not be the best way to attract a Korean man. Instead, focus on your personal qualities and values, such as kindness, intelligence, humor, and emotional maturity. These qualities can be more important than physical appearance in building a strong and lasting relationship.

3. Learn about Korean Culture and Dating Norms

Learning more about Korean culture and dating norms can also be helpful in attracting a Korean man. By understanding and appreciating Korean cultural values and norms, you can show respect and appreciation for your partner's background and perspectives.

4. Be Confident and Assertive

Confidence and assertiveness can also be attractive qualities in a partner. While Korean dating culture may value respectfulness and humility, it is also important to be confident in your own abilities and willing to express your own opinions and desires.

5. Be Willing to Communicate Openly and Honestly

Communication is a key aspect of any relationship, and this is especially true in Korean dating culture. By being willing to communicate openly and honestly with your partner, you can build trust and intimacy in your relationship.

Attracting a Korean man can be a challenging but rewarding experience. By embracing your unique qualities and cultural background, focusing on your personal qualities and values, learning about Korean culture and dating norms, being confident and assertive, and communicating openly and honestly, you can build a strong and fulfilling relationship with a Korean man. Remember to approach each relationship with an open mind and a willingness to learn and grow together, and you can create a lasting and meaningful connection.

How to Attract a Korean Man

Tips for Standing Out and Catching the Attention of a Korean Man

Attracting the attention of a Korean man can be a challenge, especially if you're unfamiliar with Korean dating culture. However, there are many ways to stand out and catch the attention of a Korean man. In this chapter, we will explore some tips for standing out and catching the attention of a Korean man.

1. Dress Stylishly and Appropriately

Korean men often place a high value on physical appearance, and dressing stylishly and appropriately can help you catch their attention. In Korean dating culture, it's important to dress conservatively and avoid overly revealing clothing, especially in the early stages of a relationship.

2. Show Interest in Korean Culture and Language

Korean men appreciate partners who are interested in Korean culture and language. By showing an interest in Korean culture and language, you can demonstrate respect for your partner's background and create opportunities for shared experiences and conversations.

3. Be Independent and Confident

Independence and confidence can also be attractive qualities in a partner. Korean men appreciate partners who are able to take care of themselves and pursue their own interests and goals. By being independent and confident, you can demonstrate that you have your own life and interests, and are not solely focused on the relationship.

4. Be Respectful and Humble

Respectfulness and humility are important values in Korean dating culture. By being respectful and humble, you can demonstrate that you are willing to learn and grow together with your partner, and are not arrogant or dismissive of their perspectives.

5. Show Interest in Your Partner's Hobbies and Interests

Korean men appreciate partners who show an interest in their hobbies and interests. By taking the time to learn about your partner's passions and activities, you can demonstrate that you are invested in their happiness and well-being.

6. Be Willing to Communicate Openly and Honestly

Communication is key in any relationship, and this is especially true in Korean dating culture. By being willing to communicate openly and honestly with your partner, you can build trust and intimacy in your relationship.

Standing out and catching the attention of a Korean man can be challenging, but it is possible with the right approach. By dressing stylishly and appropriately, showing an interest in Korean culture and language, being independent and confident, respectful and humble, showing interest in your partner's hobbies and interests, and being willing to communicate openly and honestly, you can create a strong and meaningful connection with a Korean man. Remember to approach each relationship with an open mind and a willingness to learn and grow together, and you can create a lasting and meaningful connection.

Approaches to Expressing Interest and Building a Connection

Expressing interest and building a connection with a Korean man can be challenging, especially if you're unfamiliar with Korean dating culture. However, there are many approaches you can take to express your interest and build a strong and meaningful connection. In this chapter, we will explore some approaches to expressing interest and building a connection with a Korean man.

1. Use Body Language

Body language can be a powerful tool for expressing interest and building a connection. In Korean dating culture, subtle gestures such as leaning in, making eye contact, and smiling can indicate interest and attraction.

2. Start a Conversation

Starting a conversation is a great way to express your interest and build a connection. In Korean dating culture, it's important to be respectful and considerate in your approach. Start with a friendly greeting and try to find common ground to discuss.

3. Share Your Interests and Experiences

Sharing your interests and experiences is a great way to build a connection with a Korean man. By sharing your passions and experiences, you can create opportunities for shared interests and conversations, and demonstrate your unique qualities and values.

4. Ask Open-Ended Questions

Asking open-ended questions can be a great way to build a connection and learn more about your partner. In Korean dating culture, it's important to be respectful and curious in your approach. Ask open-ended questions that encourage your partner to share their thoughts and experiences.

5. Show Your Support and Interest

Showing your support and interest can be a powerful way to build a connection with a Korean man. In Korean dating culture, it's important to be considerate and respectful in your approach. Show your support and interest by listening actively, asking thoughtful questions, and offering encouragement and support.

Strategies for Building a Strong Foundation for a Relationship

Building a strong foundation for a relationship is essential for creating a healthy and fulfilling partnership. In Korean dating culture, there are certain strategies that can be particularly effective for building a strong foundation. In this chapter, we will explore some strategies for building a strong foundation for a relationship with a Korean man.

1. Focus on Communication

Communication is the cornerstone of any successful relationship. In Korean dating culture, it's important to be open and honest in your communication, and to actively listen to your partner's perspective. By prioritizing communication, you can build trust and intimacy in your relationship, and avoid misunderstandings and conflicts.

2. Create Shared Experiences

Shared experiences can be a powerful way to build a connection and create a shared sense of identity in a relationship. In Korean dating culture, it's common to engage in shared activities such as hiking, cooking, or attending cultural events together. By creating shared experiences, you can build a sense of closeness and shared values with your partner.

3. Show Appreciation and Gratitude

Showing appreciation and gratitude can be a powerful way to strengthen a relationship. In Korean dating culture, it's important to show respect and gratitude for your partner's contributions and efforts. By expressing your appreciation and gratitude, you can create a positive and supportive atmosphere in your relationship, and build a sense of mutual respect and admiration.

4. Be Willing to Compromise

Compromise is an essential skill for any successful relationship. In Korean dating culture, it's important to be flexible and willing to compromise in order to accommodate your partner's needs and perspectives. By being willing to compromise, you can demonstrate your commitment to your relationship and create a sense of mutual respect and understanding.

5. Build Trust

Trust is essential for building a strong and healthy relationship. In Korean dating culture, trust is often built through consistent actions and behaviors that demonstrate commitment and integrity. By building trust with your partner, you can create a strong and stable foundation for your relationship.

6. Prioritize Emotional Intimacy

Emotional intimacy is an important aspect of any successful relationship. In Korean dating culture, emotional intimacy is often built through shared experiences, open communication, and mutual support. By prioritizing emotional intimacy, you can build a deep and meaningful connection with your partner, and create a sense of mutual trust and understanding.

Building a strong foundation for a relationship with a Korean man requires a commitment to communication, shared experiences, appreciation and gratitude, compromise, trust, and emotional intimacy. By prioritizing these strategies, you can create a healthy and fulfilling partnership that is grounded in mutual respect, understanding, and support. Remember to approach each relationship with an open mind and a willingness to learn and grow together, and you can build a lasting and meaningful connection with a Korean man.

How to Keep a Korean Man

Keys to Building a Strong, Healthy, and Fulfilling Relationship with a Korean Man

Building a strong, healthy, and fulfilling relationship with a Korean man can be a rewarding and enriching experience. However, it requires effort, commitment, and an understanding of Korean dating culture. In this chapter, we will explore some key strategies for building a strong, healthy, and fulfilling relationship with a Korean man.

1. Mutual Respect and Understanding

Mutual respect and understanding are essential for any successful relationship. In Korean dating culture, it's important to be respectful of your partner's beliefs, values, and cultural background. By demonstrating a willingness to learn and understand your partner's perspective, you can build a strong foundation for your relationship and avoid misunderstandings and conflicts.

2. Open Communication

Open communication is essential for building trust and intimacy in a relationship. In Korean dating culture, it's important to be honest and transparent in your communication, and to actively listen to your partner's perspective. By prioritizing communication, you can build a strong and meaningful connection with your partner, and avoid misunderstandings and conflicts.

3. Emotional Support

Emotional support is an important aspect of any successful relationship. In Korean dating culture, emotional support is often demonstrated through shared experiences, open communication, and mutual understanding. By offering emotional support to your partner, you can build a deep and meaningful connection, and create a sense of mutual trust and understanding.

4. Shared Goals and Values

Shared goals and values are important for building a sense of unity and purpose in a relationship. In Korean dating culture, it's common for couples to share similar values and aspirations, such as family, education, and career success. By aligning your goals and values with your partner's, you can create a sense of shared purpose and direction in your relationship.

5. Flexibility and Compromise

Flexibility and compromise are essential skills for any successful relationship. In Korean dating culture, it's important to be flexible and willing to compromise in order to accommodate your partner's needs and perspectives. By being willing to compromise, you can demonstrate your commitment to your relationship and create a sense of mutual respect and understanding.

6. Shared Experiences

Shared experiences can be a powerful way to build a connection and create a shared sense of identity in a relationship. In Korean dating culture, it's common to engage in shared activities such as hiking, cooking, or attending cultural events together. By creating shared experiences, you can build a sense of closeness and shared values with your partner.

Building a strong, healthy, and fulfilling relationship with a Korean man requires a commitment to mutual respect and understanding, open communication, emotional support, shared goals and values, flexibility and compromise, and shared experiences. By prioritizing these strategies, you can create a healthy and fulfilling partnership that is grounded in mutual respect, understanding, and support. Remember to approach each relationship with an open mind and a willingness to learn and grow together, and you can build a lasting and meaningful connection with a Korean man.

Strategies for Navigating Cultural Differences and Communication Challenges

Dating a Korean man can be a rich and rewarding experience, but it also comes with its own set of challenges. Cultural differences and communication challenges can arise, making it important to approach the relationship with an open mind and a willingness to learn and grow together. In this chapter, we will explore some strategies for navigating these challenges and building a strong, healthy, and fulfilling relationship with your Korean partner.

1. Understand the Importance of Culture

Understanding the importance of culture in Korean dating is essential for navigating cultural differences. Korean culture is deeply rooted in tradition and values, which can impact everything from communication style to gender roles. Take the time to learn about your partner's cultural background, beliefs, and values, and be respectful of their traditions and practices.

2. Practice Active Listening

Active listening is an important tool for effective communication in any relationship. When communicating with your Korean partner, make sure to actively listen to their perspective and take the time to understand their point of view. Avoid making assumptions or jumping to conclusions, and seek clarification when needed.

3. Embrace Language Learning

Learning Korean language can help you to communicate better with your partner and build a stronger connection. While it may be challenging to learn a new language, it can also be a fun and rewarding experience. Take classes or use language learning apps to improve your skills, and practice with your partner regularly.

4. Be Open to Compromise

Compromise is key to any successful relationship, especially when navigating cultural differences. Be open to compromising on certain beliefs or practices, and be willing to find a middle ground that works for both you and your partner.

5. Take Time to Reflect

Taking time to reflect on your own cultural background and biases can help you to better understand and appreciate your partner's culture. Consider how your own cultural background may impact your perspective, and be open to questioning your own assumptions and biases.

6. Seek Support

Navigating cultural differences and communication challenges can be difficult, so it's important to seek support when needed. Talk to friends or family members who may have experience with intercultural relationships, or seek out resources online or in your community.

Navigating cultural differences and communication challenges in a relationship with a Korean man can be challenging, but with the right strategies and mindset, it can also be a rewarding and enriching experience. By understanding the importance of culture, practicing active listening, embracing language learning, being open to compromise, taking time to reflect, and seeking support, you can build a strong and meaningful connection with your partner. Remember to approach the relationship with an open mind and a willingness to learn and grow together, and you can navigate any challenge that comes your way.

Tips for Sustaining Passion and Keeping the Relationship Fresh Over Time

Maintaining a strong and healthy relationship with a Korean man takes effort and dedication. As time goes on, it can be easy to fall into routines and lose the passion that was once present in the relationship. In this chapter, we will explore some tips for sustaining passion and keeping the relationship fresh over time.

1. Prioritize Quality Time

One of the most important aspects of sustaining passion in a relationship is prioritizing quality time together. Make time for date nights, weekend getaways, and other activities that allow you to connect and enjoy each other's company.

2. Communicate Your Needs

Effective communication is key to any successful relationship, and this is especially true when it comes to sustaining passion. Make sure to communicate your needs and desires to your partner, and be open to hearing their needs as well. This can help you both to feel heard and appreciated, which can in turn help to sustain the passion in the relationship.

3. Explore New Activities Together

Trying new things together can help to keep the relationship fresh and exciting. Whether it's trying a new restaurant, taking a dance class, or planning a weekend getaway, exploring new activities together can help to reignite the passion in your relationship.

4. Show Affection and Appreciation

Showing affection and appreciation for your partner is important for keeping the relationship strong and sustaining passion. Make sure to regularly express your love and appreciation for your partner, whether it's through verbal affirmations, physical touch, or small gestures of kindness.

5. Keep Things Spontaneous

Adding an element of spontaneity to your relationship can help to keep things fresh and exciting. Surprise your partner with a thoughtful gift, plan a spontaneous weekend getaway, or simply take them out for a surprise date night.

6. Practice Self-Care

Taking care of yourself is an important aspect of maintaining passion in a relationship. Make sure to prioritize self-care activities, such as exercise, meditation, or hobbies that you enjoy. When you feel good about yourself, you are more likely to be present and engaged in your relationship, which can help to sustain passion over time.

Sustaining passion and keeping the relationship fresh over time takes effort and dedication, but it is possible with the right mindset and strategies. Prioritizing quality time together, communicating your needs, exploring new activities together, showing affection and appreciation, keeping things spontaneous, and practicing self-care are all important tips for sustaining passion and keeping the relationship strong over time. Remember to approach the relationship with an open mind and a willingness to grow and evolve together, and you can build a long-lasting and fulfilling relationship with your Korean partner.

Overcoming Challenges in a Korean-Western Relationship

Common Challenges Faced by Korean-Western Couples

While relationships between Korean and Western partners can be incredibly fulfilling, they also come with their own set of unique challenges. In this chapter, we will explore some of the common challenges faced by Korean-Western couples and offer strategies for overcoming them.

1. Cultural Differences

One of the biggest challenges faced by Korean-Western couples is the cultural differences between the two partners. Each culture has its own values, customs, and traditions, and navigating these differences can be challenging. It's important to approach these differences with an open mind and a willingness to learn and understand each other's cultures.

2. Language Barriers

Language barriers can also be a major challenge in Korean-Western relationships. Communication is key to any successful relationship, and when partners speak different languages, it can be difficult to fully express their thoughts and feelings. It's important to be patient with each other and to work together to improve communication skills.

3. Family Expectations

Family expectations can also be a challenge in Korean-Western relationships, particularly when it comes to marriage and children. In Korean culture, there is often a strong emphasis on family and the importance of carrying on the family line. Western partners may have different expectations or timelines for these milestones, which can lead to tension and conflict. It's important to have open and honest conversations about these expectations and to find a compromise that works for both partners.

4. Stereotypes and Prejudices

Unfortunately, Korean-Western couples may also face stereotypes and prejudices from others. These can include assumptions about the relationship dynamic, cultural differences, and even racist attitudes. It's important for partners to support each other and to stand up against any discrimination they may face.

5. Long-Distance Relationships

Many Korean-Western couples may also face the challenge of long-distance relationships. This can be difficult, as it requires a lot of patience, trust, and communication to maintain a strong connection across distance and time zones. It's important to establish clear communication channels and to make an effort to visit each other as often as possible.

Strategies for Overcoming Challenges and Building a Successful Relationship

While there are many challenges that can arise in Korean-Western relationships, there are also many strategies that can help couples overcome these obstacles and build a successful relationship. In this chapter, we will explore some of the key strategies for building a strong, healthy, and fulfilling relationship with a Korean partner.

1. Communication is Key

One of the most important strategies for building a successful relationship with a Korean partner is to prioritize communication. This means not only being open and honest with each other, but also actively listening and seeking to understand each other's perspectives. Effective communication involves both verbal and nonverbal cues, and it's important to be aware of both in order to have a successful relationship.

2. Respect Each Other's Culture

Another important strategy is to respect each other's culture. This means being willing to learn about and appreciate the values, customs, and traditions of your partner's culture. It also means being open to compromise and finding ways to incorporate elements of both cultures into your relationship.

3. Embrace Differences

Rather than seeing cultural differences as obstacles, it's important to embrace them as opportunities for growth and learning. Differences in values, beliefs, and perspectives can offer new and exciting ways of seeing the world and can help partners learn from each other.

4. Focus on Commonalities

While differences are important to embrace, it's also important to focus on the commonalities that brought you together in the first place. Shared interests, values, and goals can provide a strong foundation for a successful relationship.

5. Establish Boundaries

Establishing clear boundaries is another important strategy for building a successful relationship with a Korean partner. This means communicating your needs and expectations clearly, and being willing to respect your partner's boundaries as well.

6. Prioritize Trust

Trust is a crucial component of any successful relationship, and it's particularly important in Korean-Western relationships where there may be language or cultural barriers. Building trust involves being honest and transparent with each other, following through on commitments, and being willing to communicate openly about any concerns or issues that arise.

7. Build Strong Connections with Family

Family is often a central component of Korean culture, and building strong connections with your partner's family can be key to building a successful relationship. This means being willing to learn about and respect family traditions, as well as being willing to communicate openly with family members.

8. Celebrate Milestones Together

Celebrating milestones together can also be a great way to build a successful relationship with a Korean partner. This means celebrating important holidays and milestones from both cultures, as well as finding ways to create your own traditions and celebrations together.

9. Stay Positive and Supportive

Finally, staying positive and supportive can help build a strong and healthy relationship. This means being there for each other through both the good times and the challenging times, and being willing to support each other in pursuit of individual goals and dreams.

Building a successful relationship with a Korean partner requires patience, understanding, and a willingness to learn and grow together. By prioritizing communication, respecting each other's culture, embracing differences, focusing on commonalities, establishing boundaries, prioritizing trust, building strong connections with family, celebrating milestones together, and staying positive and supportive, couples can overcome the challenges that arise in Korean-Western relationships and build a strong and fulfilling partnership.

Navigating Cultural Differences with Empathy, Curiosity, and Respect

One of the biggest challenges that Korean-Western couples face is navigating cultural differences. These differences can manifest in a variety of ways, from communication styles and attitudes towards intimacy to expectations around family and finances. However, with empathy, curiosity, and respect, couples can work through these differences and build a strong and healthy relationship.

1. Develop Empathy

Empathy is the ability to understand and share the feelings of another person. In order to navigate cultural differences with empathy, it's important to take the time to learn about your partner's cultural background and understand how their experiences and values have shaped their perspective. This means being willing to listen with an open mind and heart, and seeking to understand your partner's point of view without judgment or criticism.

2. Approach Differences with Curiosity

Approaching cultural differences with curiosity involves asking questions and seeking to learn more about your partner's culture. This means being willing to explore differences with an open mind and a desire to learn, rather than jumping to conclusions or making assumptions. It's important to approach differences with a spirit of curiosity and a willingness to learn, rather than seeing them as obstacles or challenges.

3. Show Respect

Showing respect for your partner's culture and background is crucial for navigating cultural differences. This means being willing to learn about and appreciate your partner's traditions, values, and beliefs, even if they differ from your own. It also means being willing to compromise and find ways to incorporate elements of both cultures into your relationship.

4. Be Mindful of Language and Communication

Language and communication can be a major barrier in Korean-Western relationships. It's important to be mindful of differences in language and communication styles, and to be patient and understanding when communication difficulties arise. This means being willing to ask for clarification when needed, and being patient and understanding when your partner is struggling to express themselves.

5. Seek Out Resources and Support

Navigating cultural differences can be challenging, and it's important to seek out resources and support to help you along the way. This can include seeking out books, articles, or videos that explore Korean culture, as well as connecting with other Korean-Western couples who can share their experiences and offer support and guidance.

6. Be Willing to Compromise

Compromise is key to navigating cultural differences in a relationship. This means being willing to find common ground and make compromises in order to accommodate both partners' needs and desires. It also means being willing to explore new ways of doing things and being open to trying new things.

7. Embrace Differences

Rather than seeing cultural differences as obstacles, it's important to embrace them as opportunities for growth and learning. Differences in values, beliefs, and perspectives can offer new and exciting ways of seeing the world and can help partners learn from each other. By embracing differences with an open mind and heart, couples can build a strong and healthy relationship that transcends cultural boundaries.

Perspectives from Korean Men and their Partners

Real-Life Stories and Experiences from Korean Men and their Western Partners

Real-life stories and experiences from Korean men and their Western partners offer valuable insights into the complexities and joys of cross-cultural relationships. In this chapter, we will share some of these stories, highlighting the challenges, triumphs, and lessons learned along the way.

1. Han and Sarah

Han and Sarah met while studying abroad in the United States. Han, a Korean student studying engineering, was drawn to Sarah's warm personality and outgoing nature. As they began dating, they quickly realized that their cultural backgrounds posed significant challenges. Han struggled with expressing his emotions and often felt overwhelmed by the demands of Sarah's outgoing personality. Sarah, on the other hand, found it difficult to understand Han's reserved nature and was often frustrated by his lack of emotional expression.

Over time, Han and Sarah learned to communicate more effectively and to understand and appreciate each other's cultural differences. They worked to find common ground and to compromise when needed, and over time, they built a strong and healthy relationship based on mutual respect and understanding.

2. Sung and Emma

Sung and Emma met in Seoul, where Emma was working as an English teacher. Sung, a successful businessman, was immediately drawn to Emma's intelligence and confidence. As they began dating, they quickly realized that their different cultural backgrounds presented challenges. Sung struggled with adjusting to Emma's more assertive personality, while Emma found it difficult to navigate Sung's busy work schedule and the demands of his family.

Despite these challenges, Sung and Emma were committed to building a life together. They learned to communicate more effectively and to work together to find solutions to the challenges they faced. Over time, they built a strong and loving relationship based on mutual respect and a deep understanding of each other's cultural backgrounds.

3. Joon and Heather

Joon and Heather met in college, where they were both studying art. Joon, a Korean student, was immediately drawn to Heather's creative spirit and passion for art. As they began dating, they quickly realized that their different cultural backgrounds presented challenges. Joon struggled with understanding Heather's more liberal attitudes towards sex and relationships, while Heather found it difficult to navigate Joon's more conservative values.

Despite these challenges, Joon and Heather were committed to building a life together. They worked hard to communicate openly and honestly with each other, and to find ways to compromise and accommodate each other's needs and desires. Over time, they built a strong and loving relationship based on mutual respect and understanding.

Lessons Learned and Insights Gained from Navigating Cultural Differences and Building Successful Relationships

Navigating cultural differences in a relationship can be challenging, but it can also be incredibly rewarding. It offers an opportunity to learn about and appreciate a different culture, to grow personally and as a couple, and to build a strong and healthy relationship based on mutual respect and understanding. In this chapter, we will share some of the key lessons learned and insights gained from navigating cultural differences and building successful relationships.

1. Communication is key

Effective communication is crucial in any relationship, but it is especially important in cross-cultural relationships. In order to build a strong and healthy relationship, it is essential to communicate openly and honestly with each other, to listen actively, and to seek to understand each other's perspectives and experiences. This can involve being patient, learning to express oneself in different ways, and being willing to compromise.

2. Embrace differences with curiosity and empathy

Cultural differences can be both fascinating and challenging. Rather than trying to ignore or downplay these differences, it can be helpful to embrace them with curiosity and empathy.

This means being open to learning about and experiencing different cultural traditions, values, and norms. It also means being willing to accept and respect differences, rather than trying to change or control them.

3. Focus on building a strong foundation

Building a strong foundation for a relationship involves taking the time to get to know each other, to build trust and intimacy, and to establish shared values and goals. This can involve engaging in activities together, learning about each other's interests, and sharing experiences that help to deepen your connection.

4. Recognize the impact of cultural background on attitudes and behaviors

It is important to recognize that cultural background can have a significant impact on attitudes and behaviors, particularly in areas such as communication, intimacy, and gender roles. Understanding and respecting these differences can help to avoid misunderstandings and conflicts, and can also help to strengthen your relationship.

5. Be patient and willing to learn

Navigating cultural differences takes time and patience. It can be easy to get frustrated or discouraged when faced with challenges, but it is important to remember that building a successful cross-cultural relationship is a process that requires ongoing learning and adaptation.

Building a successful cross-cultural relationship requires patience, empathy, and a willingness to learn and adapt. By focusing on effective communication, embracing differences with curiosity and empathy, building a strong foundation, recognizing the impact of cultural background, and being patient and willing to learn, Korean-Western couples can build strong and healthy relationships that transcend cultural boundaries. While challenges are inevitable, the rewards of building a successful cross-cultural relationship are immeasurable.

Conclusion: Building a Successful Relationship with a Korean Man

Final Thoughts and Tips for Building a Successful Relationship with a Korean Man

Building a successful relationship with a Korean man can be an exciting and rewarding journey. It can also be challenging at times, particularly when navigating cultural differences and expectations. In this final chapter, we offer some additional tips and insights for building a strong and healthy relationship with a Korean man.

1. Be respectful and understanding of his cultural background

As we've discussed throughout this book, cultural background plays a significant role in shaping attitudes and behaviors. It is important to be respectful and understanding of your Korean partner's cultural background, even if it differs from your own. This means being willing to learn about and appreciate Korean culture, traditions, and values, and being open to adapting your own behavior when necessary.

2. Build trust and intimacy

Trust and intimacy are essential components of a successful relationship. This involves being honest and open with your partner, sharing your thoughts and feelings, and being willing to listen and understand his perspectives. It can also involve physical touch, affection, and intimacy, which can help to deepen your connection and build a stronger bond.

3. Focus on shared interests and goals

While it's important to respect and appreciate each other's differences, it's also important to focus on shared interests and goals. This can involve finding common hobbies or activities to engage in together, or setting shared goals that you can work towards as a couple. This helps to build a sense of shared purpose and unity, and can also help to deepen your connection.

4. Be patient and understanding

As with any relationship, it's important to be patient and understanding with your Korean partner. This means being willing to communicate openly and honestly, even when faced with challenges or misunderstandings. It also means being willing to compromise and adapt your behavior when necessary, and being supportive and understanding of your partner's needs and feelings.

5. Celebrate your love and your relationship

Finally, it's important to celebrate your love and your relationship, and to embrace all of the wonderful experiences and moments that come with being in a loving and committed partnership. Whether it's a special date night, a romantic getaway, or simply taking the time to appreciate each other's company, make sure to take time to celebrate your love and to cherish the moments that you share together.

Building a successful relationship with a Korean man can be a challenging, yet rewarding journey. By focusing on respect, trust, intimacy, shared interests and goals, patience, and celebration, Korean-Western couples can build strong and healthy relationships that transcend cultural boundaries. Remember to always communicate openly and honestly, be willing to learn and adapt, and most importantly, cherish and celebrate the love that you share.

Recap of Key Takeaways and Insights from the Book

Throughout this book, we've explored the unique cultural and social factors that influence Korean men and their attitudes towards dating, relationships, intimacy, and marriage. We've also provided practical tips and insights for navigating cultural differences, building strong and healthy relationships, and overcoming challenges that may arise along the way. In this final chapter, we recap some of the key takeaways and insights from the book.

1. Cultural background plays a significant role in shaping attitudes and behaviors.

As we've discussed throughout the book, cultural background plays a significant role in shaping Korean men's attitudes towards dating, relationships, intimacy, and marriage. It's important for non-Korean partners to be respectful and understanding of their partner's cultural background, and to be willing to learn and adapt as necessary.

2. Communication and trust are essential for building a successful relationship.

Trust and open communication are essential components of a successful relationship. This involves being honest and open with your partner, sharing your thoughts and feelings, and being willing to listen and understand his perspectives. It can also involve physical touch, affection, and intimacy, which can help to deepen your connection and build a stronger bond.

3. Traditional gender roles and expectations still play a significant role in Korean relationships.

While attitudes and expectations around gender roles and relationships are evolving in Korean culture, traditional gender roles and expectations still play a significant role in many Korean relationships. It's important for non-Korean partners to be aware of these expectations and to be willing to navigate them with empathy and understanding.

4. Navigating cultural differences can be challenging but rewarding.

Navigating cultural differences in a relationship can be challenging, but it can also be incredibly rewarding. By approaching cultural differences with empathy, curiosity, and respect, non-Korean partners can gain a deeper appreciation and understanding of Korean culture, and build stronger relationships as a result.

5. Building a successful relationship takes effort and patience.

Building a successful relationship with a Korean man takes effort, patience, and a willingness to adapt and compromise. It's important to be patient, understanding, and supportive of your partner's needs and feelings, and to work together to build a strong and healthy relationship that transcends cultural boundaries.

Encouragement to Approach Dating and Relationships with an Open Mind and Cultural Sensitivity

As we come to the end of this book, it's important to emphasize the importance of approaching dating and relationships with an open mind and cultural sensitivity. While it can be easy to fall into stereotypes and assumptions about other cultures, doing so can limit our ability to build strong and healthy relationships that transcend cultural boundaries. In this chapter, we'll explore why it's important to approach dating and relationships with cultural sensitivity, and offer encouragement for those who are embarking on this exciting and challenging journey.

Why Cultural Sensitivity Matters in Dating and Relationships

Cultural sensitivity is important in dating and relationships for several reasons. Firstly, it helps to build trust and mutual understanding between partners. When we approach our partners with empathy, curiosity, and respect for their cultural background, we're better able to connect with them on a deeper level, and to build trust and intimacy over time.

Secondly, cultural sensitivity helps to break down stereotypes and assumptions about other cultures. By taking the time to learn about our partner's cultural background, we can gain a deeper appreciation and understanding of their unique experiences, values, and perspectives. This, in turn, can help us to challenge our own assumptions and biases, and to build more meaningful and fulfilling relationships.

Finally, cultural sensitivity helps to promote mutual respect and inclusivity in our relationships. When we approach our partners with cultural sensitivity, we're sending the message that we value and respect their cultural background, and that we're willing to work together to build a relationship that honors both of our unique perspectives and experiences.

Encouragement for Approaching Dating and Relationships with Cultural Sensitivity

Approaching dating and relationships with cultural sensitivity can be challenging, but it can also be incredibly rewarding. Here are a few tips and words of encouragement for those who are embarking on this exciting and challenging journey:

1. Be open-minded and curious: When you approach dating and relationships with an open mind and a curious spirit, you're better able to learn from your partner's unique experiences and perspectives. This can help you to build a deeper connection with your partner, and to challenge your own assumptions and biases about other cultures.
2. Embrace differences: Differences in culture, personality, and background can be challenging at times, but they can also be incredibly enriching. By embracing these differences and working together to find common ground, you can build a relationship that honors both of your unique perspectives and experiences.
3. Practice empathy and active listening: When you practice empathy and active listening in your relationship, you're better able to understand and

connect with your partner's experiences and perspectives. This, in turn, can help you to build trust and intimacy over time.

4. Be patient and understanding: Building a successful relationship takes time, patience, and understanding. Be patient with your partner as you navigate cultural differences and challenges, and be willing to listen and adapt as necessary.

5. Celebrate your differences: Instead of viewing cultural differences as a barrier, try to celebrate them as a unique and enriching aspect of your relationship. By celebrating your differences, you can build a relationship that's truly one-of-a-kind.

Final words of advice for building a happy and fulfilling relationship with a Korean man

As we come to the end of this book, it's important to remember that building a successful relationship with a Korean man is not just about following a set of rules or cultural norms. It's about creating a connection with another person based on mutual respect, understanding, and empathy.

One of the most important pieces of advice that we can offer is to approach your relationship with an open mind and a willingness to learn. Cultural differences may present challenges, but they can also provide opportunities for growth and understanding.

It's also important to remember that every individual is unique, regardless of their cultural background. While we have provided insights and generalizations throughout this book, it's crucial to approach each person as an individual with their own preferences and needs.

Communication is key in any relationship, and this is especially true when navigating cultural differences. Take the time to listen to your partner and communicate your own thoughts and feelings clearly and respectfully. Don't be afraid to ask questions and seek clarification if needed.

Another important aspect of building a happy and fulfilling relationship with a Korean man is to prioritize trust and honesty. This includes being transparent about your own feelings, goals, and intentions, as well as being willing to trust your partner and work together towards a shared vision for your future.

Finally, remember to prioritize self-care and personal growth as well. A healthy and fulfilling relationship requires two healthy and fulfilled individuals. Make time for your own hobbies, interests, and self-reflection, and continue to learn and grow as an individual even as you build a life together with your partner.

We hope that this book has provided you with valuable insights and strategies for building a successful relationship with a Korean man. Remember to approach each new experience with curiosity, empathy, and an open heart, and we wish you all the best on your journey towards love and happiness.

Thank you for taking the time to read our book about dating and building relationships with Korean men. We hope that you found it informative, engaging, and helpful in navigating the complexities of cross-cultural relationships.

If you enjoyed reading our book and found it helpful, we would greatly appreciate it if you could leave a positive review on the platform where you purchased it. Your feedback is important to us and will help others who may be interested in this topic discover our book and benefit from our insights and experiences.

Once again, thank you for choosing to read our book. We wish you all the best in your journey towards building a happy and fulfilling relationship with a Korean man.

Printed in Great Britain
by Amazon